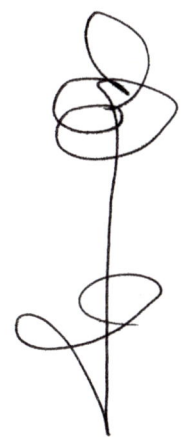

Signs of Early Man

Jane Weir

Templar Poetry

First Published 2009 by Templar Poetry
Templar Poetry is an imprint of Delamide & Bell

Fenelon House
Kingsbridge Terrace
58 Dale Road, Matlock, Derbyshire
DE4 3NB

www.templarpoetry.co.uk

ISBN 978-1-906285128

Copyright © Jane Weir 2009

Jane Weir has asserted her moral right to be identified as the author
of this work in accordance
with the Copyright, Designs and Patents Act 1988

All rights reserved. This book is sold subject to the condition
that it shall not, by way of trade or otherwise, be lent, resold, hired out
or otherwise circulated without the publisher's prior consent, in any form
of binding or cover other than that in which it is published and without
a similar condition including this condition being imposed on
the subsequent purchaser.

For permission to reprint or broadcast these poems write to
Templar Poetry

A CIP catalogue record of this book is available from the British Library.

Typeset by Pliny
Graphics by Paloma Violet
Printed and bound in India

Also by Jane Weir

Poetry

The Way I Dressed During the Revolution (2005)
Alice (2006)
Before Playing Romeo (2007)
Walking the Block (2008)

Monograph

Charlotte Mew: Between the Dome and the Stars (2007)

For Dorothy

Contents

Simply Sat At The Foot, Tissington	1
The David Mellor Kitchen Shop Reverie	2
Stood at Alan Bate's Grave	3
Our Conversation About Spider Webs	4
After a Lecture at Hardwick Hall On Seventeenth Century Embroidery	5
The Two of us Talking About Otto and Jake	7
To Fold the Shutters, Ravendale	9
We Discuss D. H. Lawrence's Story, *The Fox*	10
The English Talent for Toads	12

Toy Box Open

From Out of a Lever Came a Doll of Sorts	14
Points to Consider When Making an Effigy	15
Poppet	16
The Folk Rook Stuffing	17
Indian Elephant Named 'Socks'	18
Happy Sock, Happy Glove, Happy Cat	19
Folk Owl	20
Linocut Weasel	22
Snout of The Mole	23
Nasturtium Seed	24

Toy Box Closed

Hen	26
Magpie Husbandry	28
In Three Acts: Jane and Dorothy Fold Pieces of Pea Green Linen Printed With Cow Parsley	29
A Turnip for Blue John	30
Crich With Sunbeams and Pewter Showers	31
Margaret	32
The Door is Grey	33

Simply Sat at The Foot, Tissington

Spring has begun to draw out buds, bud by bud,
as fingers slip, one by one out of kid gloves, bud by bud by bud.
Buds drawn down through greens,
buds in pink-white, green-white, yellow-white,
opening as we sit, hands clasped like sponge ware
around the kitchen table. Two legs propped
to stop the wobble, by copies of *The Rainbow* and *The Fox*.

Looking out over a swatch of garden,
over the higgledy piggle of dry stone walls,
over the silent, for a second, no more than a second,
over the silent road, free from curlew, free from grouse,
over palettes of fields, where oddly spaced sheep graze
among chokes of thistles, stakes of teasels.

We're both waiting, as a newly planted wood waits
to sear the tip of the sky. Both waiting, waiting for the same,
waiting for different things, both of us thinking,
thinking different things, thinking the same things,
trying not to think, trying not to feel, trying not to think,
to feel, yet thinking, feeling, imagining a day, a night,
when grubs turn full circle inside our apple heads,
and nothing but a lapwing bats an eyelid.

The David Mellor Kitchen Shop Reverie

It's not often I allow myself
the luxury of a new brush.
But the sight of an aisle free from clutter,
equipment minimised, crockery
in its proper place, makes me leap.

In a shallow wicker basket
I uncover the brushes of my dreams.
On every handle a choir sings out,
'Made in England by H.G. Rant.'
I know I have to pace myself,
so I strut in black Cubans
down a road of quarry tiles,
savouring like herbs the names.

Round Pastry Brush, Small Pastry Brush.
Bottle Brush, Teapot Brush
with twisted wire handle,
Pot Brush made from natural bristle,
beech topped, Flask Brush, Vegetable Brush,
two coarse, one fine, Basting Brush,
Mushroom Brush, Clothes Brush.

On the stroke of midnight, I light a tea light
for the tiny miracle of the Oil Brush,
blonde bristles of a patron saint,
buffeting the figure of an hourglass.

Stood at Alan Bate's Grave.

All this talk of *Women In Love*,
and yes we both agreed
that marriage was the end
of experience as we knew it.

Impromptu, we turned off the road,
drove into Bradbourne to see his grave.
I held this vision of *Crich*'s eyes,
glittering with fierce malignancy,
and sweat in all its clearness
stippling the slippery slopes of *Birkin's* thighs.
How Lawrence would have cackled!

Nevertheless, we stood awhile,
daffodils wilting in the sun, snowdrops
ducking into green, overhead a wedge
of woodpigeon sky splattered black with rooks.
You said, *look at that view, you'd rise every day for that.*

And I looked, as if I'd just discovered how to,
feeling the richness of your hand
dwell upon the dell of my back.
Inside the cottage we drank Taylor's tea,
ate boiled fruit cake, gazed into the firelight,
talked some sense into ourselves.

Our Conversation About Spider Webs

started because you were trying to figure out
how you might set about weaving one.
You said, 'If only I could get inside a spider's head.
– Alright! Inside its what's it called.'
Biology was never your strong point.

You said, 'If only she wasn't dead, that New England Woman
named Ruth, she might be able to shed some light.
So many arrows to her bow, laundered, cooked
baked and cleaned, spun and sewed.
By all accounts she was thick with spiders,
carded tow, wove a woollen web for aprons,
linen web for shirting, blue check for smocks.'

I grabbed the steering wheel because by now we were
scooting towards a dry stone wall and death,
though you barely noticed because Peter Collingwood
had said to come round and talk about the possibilities.

Peter Collingwood was a pioneering weaver, he wrote numerous books on the techniques and structure of rug weaving, specifically the classic *Technique Of Rug Weaving* and *The Maker's Hand: A Closer Look at Textile Structure*.

After a Lecture at Hardwick Hall
on Seventeenth Century Embroidery

the two of us were bursting
with schemes of swan bills
threaded with honesty,
of white winter hares and bulging stags,
of Eden complete with Adam and Eve,
serpent and red apple,
of *Hardwick's Inventories, 1601*:

Five pieces of hangings…
set with trees and slips and Griphons
and *a footstool of oring tawnie velvet*
set with nedleworke slips and oring tawnie frenge.

Of bed chamber hangings,
probably worked by Mary
during her imprisonment,
and to our delight slips
caught by the light with heels showing.

Ecstatic, we took the long way home,
twisting through Beeley village
because there was something
I wanted to show you;
and it didn't matter that the river
was high, high as a pair of Cavalier boots,
or that the herons nesting in the breeze
were as delicate as smoke damaged chandelier glass,
because I wanted to show you
a dwelling or rather the detail of a dwelling,
lead braces across its windowpanes;

and if our luck was in and the light held,
high mass beneath a Hopton window ledge,
the off-chance of seeing a pheasant kiss a partridge,
with what I'd term stump-work
but you, ever a stickler, would call strips
of seventeenth century raised-work.

Slips are embroidered motifs, usually in the form of a plant or flowers, with the heel or the base showing.

The quotation is from *The Inventories at Hardwick Hall Derbyshire, 1601*, (Clabburn)

The Two of us Talking About Otto and Jake

It's so easy, the two of us sitting,
talking at the edge of Over Haddon,
the engine whirr turned off,
the wood on the hill signed *Carrington*,
two of us talking about the sheer romance,
expanse of prairie men,
such as Otto and Jake in *My Antonia*.

How Jake made a snowfield
from cotton wool,
a frozen lake from his pocket mirror,
while Otto loved children,
nothing better than playing with babies,
though he had a temper.
How occasionally one or the other
would forget themselves
and swear in front of the elder women,
and the crow women would dead-eye them both,
as if they were wild boys from over Olsen's place,
caught red handed,
interfering with a palomino colt.

How they sat beneath waterfalls of oil lamplight,
telling tales of grey wolves in the Rockies,
or wildcats in Virginia,
the voyage to America.
Some nights talk turned to
how they held a spade, a rake, a sieve
mended seasoned tools around an iron stove.
And how work was epic, never ending
like the leather belts that corralled
the loops of their indigo workware,
and how work turned all mean cactus tough.

Yet God!
When the prairie grass whispered
light rippled violet across a snow field

Now as dusk fell, hissing a spell
our speech slowly teetered.
Yep, we closed the dog-eared book on them,
knowing they'd never get on somehow or make much.

My Antonia is a novel by Willa Cather about immigrant experience.

To Fold the Shutters, Ravensdale

Dark hemming darkness as we arrive.
The street, if that's what you'd call it,
though it's more an extended ginnel,
is a rock throw from the gorge's edge.
We're below a steel river sabreing
along stinking banks of wild garlic.
As if ready to dance, the mill workers'
cottages stand facing. The grass
that once sprang between has gone,
as has the old man you once spoke to
whittling a dog fox on his doorstep.
Your cottage, like a match head
strikes the end of the row.
All is still, except for the daws chuffing,
buffeting like Bedouin tents.
Nothing bobs or slants behind window glass.
We stand outside for a long time,
before we step inside. Together
we fold the shutters in a slow Pennsylvanian way.
To hand a table, the decoy of a cream
enamelware bowl, peony head of muslin
flecked with lavender, caraway seeds,
a stiff brush willing to scrub.
You're like a cuckoo clock tonight.
Through the unlatched door I watch you
on the hour, coming and going,
coming and going, until, like midnight,
your dead sure, turn to face the distemper wall,
your wedding portrait of thirty years,
stiff watercolour executed on board,
in the lolly pop style
of his Exselenc Georg General Waschingdon
and Ledy Waschingdon,
circa seventeen seventy five to eighteen hundred.

We Discuss D. H. Lawrence's Story, *The Fox*

I talk about how I almost believed…

You said it must have been
the dapple of the woods the stranger brought in,
dapple being invasive as well as sly and persuasive,
and knowing how the pine trees crouch blackly.

But I said no, it was more than that,
unable to pin down,
there was always the suspicion
of a dud inside the melody of the firelight.

To settle, we set the scenario up, rolled the dice.
I played *Bamford* you played *March*.
Both of us in our mans' overcoats,
breeched and booted, we sat contemplating.
This brought immediacy to the forefront.
What would we have done when faced?

You made up some excuse when we both knew.
I let you do what you had to do,
which was fetch the wood from the wood shed,
while I prepared the feed for the Plymouths
and Wyandottes before warming the teapot.

Turning down the bed,
such a gorgeous marshmallow white,
you made the best of *Sons and Lovers*,
sulphur daffodils, brilliant deathbed .
I watched your breasts swing as you dropped your shift
and thought of our Lurcher bitch suckling her pups,
by the crumpled orange of a dying range.

Inside my head, his words came hard, came fast,
filled my mouth, in all the heat, came up beautiful.
'Thin little wild crocuses mauve and striped,
The narcissi hung their winter stars.'

I swallowed hard, you sighed; in the copse a triangle shifted.
Ghirlanda's in bed, I reflected on how he would have loved
this or not loved this, depending on the thickness of his mood.

The dark was tough on us. I made a last stab
as streaks faded and starlight shuttered.
You became pragmatic saying,
'Well then, that's Lawrence, one hand held out,
making a flower show, the other clenched,
quick jab in our faces with his fist.'

Then we kissed.

The English Talent for Toads

I say, 'What's so hilarious
about being in the garden staking lupins?'
You say, 'That's what!'
point to an olive toad
reeling from the compost bin.
The toad, Chaucerian,
its finish coarse as a Medieval vessel,
as it slumps on the gravel.
I think, this is eccentric,
a very English incident.
Very good! Very Funny! Ha Ha!
Though you've a naïve eye.
The Italians have a word,
they call what you have *talento*.
Your English potters have *talento* too,
have a raucous sense of humour,
produce legendary jugs, mugs
with toads and frogs inside,
and master potters pierce bodkin
holes in rims, through handles,
making mugs hard to drink from,
hard to hold without spilling.
'Please explain this joke to me?'

Toy Box Open

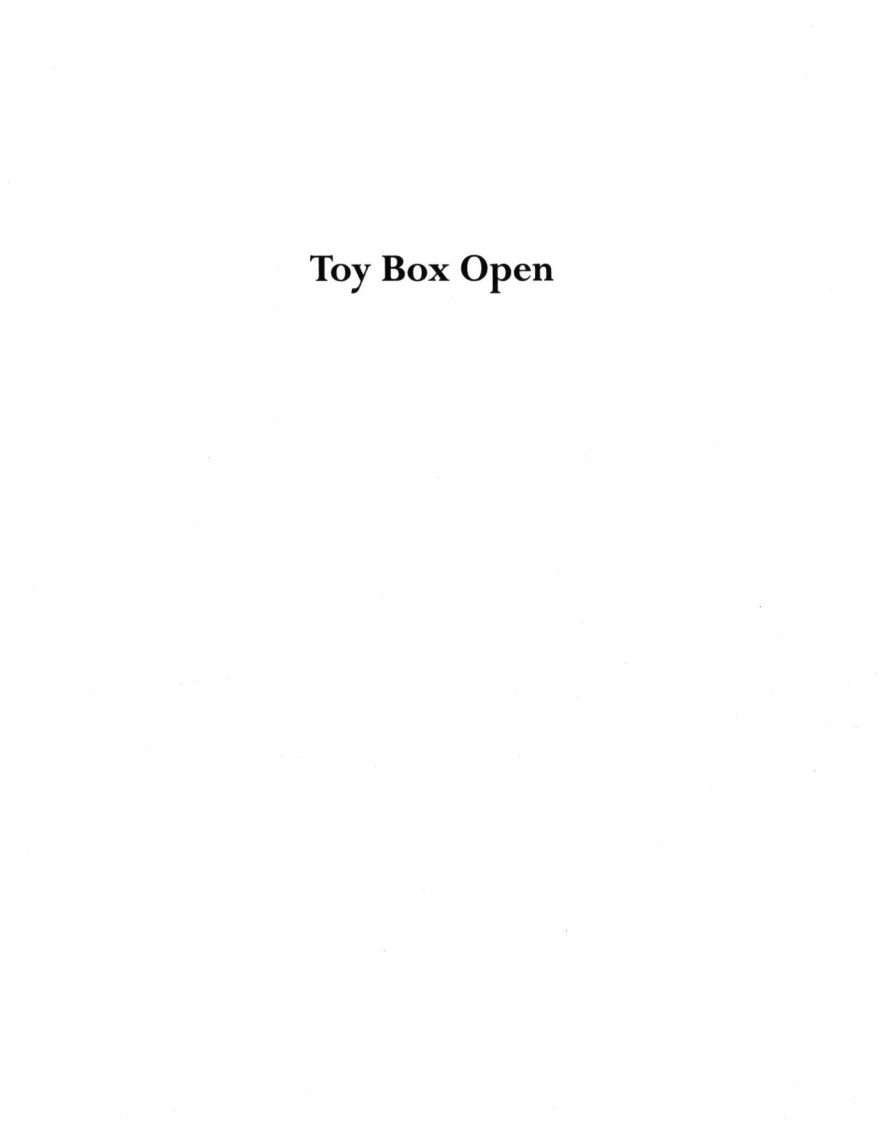

From Out of a Lever Came a Doll of Sorts

Defunct, I straddled the brick-making machine.
One hand held the lever while the other sawed.
Two minutes was all it took before hitting the slate floor.

I could have been Judith hacking off the head of Holfernes,
features of sorts protruded from the grain
and there were stubborn stains, splashes
where a can of garage floor-red backlashed red,
when poured into a handyman's can.

I handed it over saying sorry it's not Lord or Lady Clapham,
but surely there's something you could do, couldn't you?
There's something striving to get through.

'Oh yes', you said, and I could see stonemason's tools
wheeling inside the mill stone grit of your eyes.
Oh, I could see the making of a stiff jointed body,
beginnings of an intricate linen wig,
dressed in Huguenot silk, wasp-waisted.

And I know I shouldn't build up hope
faced with such a surface.
But didn't I just hear you say,
'Ah, I spy it lurking inside the holy grail of the wood.'

Lord and Lady Clapham are eighteenth century dolls.

Points to Consider When Making an Effigy

Ugly

You made up her face from plaster of paris,
by a fluke dropped her on the floor.
on examination you liked her better
now the nose was busted, mouth, jaw line corrupted,
for you could see her tiny peggies,
peggies the like of you'd never seen before,
protruding from her splintered jaw like tuiti fruity.

Neck

The doll's neck's so long you suggest a choker
to break the space. I butt in, offer a black
satin ribbon, studded with dead calamine heads.
You shake your head. You were thinking
of something less formal, something loose,
oozing decadence, because to the average punter
this was wood, not flesh.

Poppet

For eyes, two rusty nails.
For lips, two Stanley knife slashes.
The nose is a gift to the power
of the imagination.
For hair, it's a quick sojourn
across the drowsy fields,
to gather clumps of matted sheep fleece.
Beneath a throw of candlelight
you show me,
how to glue,
mount the fleece onto its head,
how to tease out strands
so they wisp and dangle.
Finally, when the wicks are snuffed
we mount the crooked stairs,
to a feather bed and sweet, sweet oblivion.
Downstairs wolf spiders
will scurry, scour and fix,
like leggy pubescent girls,
a set of stabbing hair grips.

Poppet: refers to folk magic. A doll is made to represent a person, where upon spells are cast.

The Folk Rook Stuffing

We try to imagine
the Folk Rook
without its bitter blackness,
stripped down to base-linen,
torso, legs, wings, beak.
We try to imagine
the eyes peeled off,
glazing on a white plate.

We are keen to know
what's packed inside,
what keeps the torso, legs,
wings, beak so firmly staked,
what holds the button string,
keeps the wings from flapping.
We think some sort
of homemade stuffing,
infected with charms,
though we can't be sure and argue.

I say, if it was a mole
we'd be all right,
its feet hung out
until they dried,
cure for your rheumatism.
What's with the look!

You threaten to boil the rook,
split down the middle like a haggis,
convinced badness lurks.
We rummage, skull of a wood mouse,
sliver of mandrake,
ten hairs each off our heads,
endless skins we shed.

Indian Elephant Named 'Socks'

When is a pair of speckled walking socks
no longer a pair of socks?
When ridged heels and toes are cut at an exact angle
to make Indian Elephant ears, and a strip, double-sided,
from the knee top is cut and folded, hemmed down
each side to make a trunk, and the cabled length
that stretches up the back calf, front shins
turned inside out, shaped to make
the elephants torso; and this bits a bugger
to shape when stuffed with kapok;
but its do-able, if you have a saint's patience.
The fiddly bits are the trunk, ears, tail,
the easy bits darning on the face
with what you imagine will be
the expression of a small child.

Happy Sock, Happy Glove, Happy Cat

While following *Miyako Kangmori's* sock pattern for a cat, it soon became apparent that my interpretation of cat was different from her Japanese interpretation of cat. My possible mistakes; a man's walking sock, swapped at the last minute for a woman's glove, or going for an oatmeal knit instead of solid black, favouring felt eyes over buttons for a more humane expression. Who knows, who cares? The sock's wool not stone. So there's no such thing as mistake, especially when the makings all about individual interpretation, for the sock was chosen for its flexibility. Who's to say what shape it takes, when by extension it's freely made. According to the fifteenth century *Boke of St Albans*, 'a good grey hound should have a head like a snake, the foot like a cat, the tail like a rat, the side like a bream and the back like a beam.' What says the cat?

Happy Sock and Happy Glove is a book about making toys from socks and gloves by Miyako Kangmori.

Folk Owl

He shuffled into the shed
messenger bag slung around his waist.
He wore a tweed waistcoat,
half unbuttoned cotton shirt,
boilerman's jacket.
He flipped the bag flap
causing the shed to reel.
Angle grinders ground their teeth,
time served tools wobbled like fairground skittles.

A mutt barked. A mouse squeaked
in a pile of oily shavings.
In the hamlet lights were warming up,
going on, going off,
as if they were the support act
before the darkness billed.

I remember the dull yellow
thickening of his hands.
Mustard calluses protruding
like the centre of Michaelmass daisies,
and between the breech
of his thumb, index finger,
this habit he had of rubbing
cord whilst saying nothing.

Finished with farming,
he carved country birds,
plotting their course by way of the wind,
loving the way the rooks skimmed,
like wet plaster, kestrels hitched
the broad waistband of the sky.

It's hard to comprehend,
seeing his owl staked in his fist,
for his owl is how his owl is.
I was high, electrified, having heard
no technical books on this exist.
I was drunk on the naïve, primitive.
The way he whittled the stump
scoured for burrs, knots and blemishes,
clinched traits,
for his owl is how his owl is.

We passed the time of day.
At one point the owl spun its head.
When he said, 'Go on tek it, tek it',
momentarily there was some optical confusion.

Linocut Weasel

There was always some excuse,
the linoleum wasn't right, too cold,
or the basic colour too grey, too brown;
as if that made a difference.
Or the size of the lino wasn't quite right,
too small, too big, too thin, too thick,
or you couldn't find the right pencil,
gouge, craft knife sharp enough.

Apparently, you felt confident
when cutting hares leaping,
because you'd worked out beforehand
the quantity of energy needed to capture
the creature's arcs, sinews and verve.
It was the same with crows.
For weeks you sat with a notebook and pencil
in the desolate car parks of country parks,
mounted the grass verge by The Gates at Tissington,
until you trapped their serrated lines
like tent flap wings, persian indigo,
lifting – landing – lifting – landing.
.
When it came down to the nitty-gritty
of cutting a weasel your mouth became
a crystal stopper, hands refused to decant.
I believe it wasn't the drawing or cutting,
not really, for your skill was phenomenal.
No, I'm certain it was the Lamiae coil
of the creature's Houdini body, sheer might,
fight to stake it down, hassle of the repeat,
belief that its snarl, if captured wrongly,
would, beneath lamplight, turn full circle.

Snout of The Mole

The puzzle of a bulrush,
seen protruding
from a discarded down pipe,
is in fact a common mole.
We can tell this by its paddle legs,
snout biro-ing. If it were dead,
and it will be soon if it's not released,
we could take it inside, coolly slice
a horizontal section of its dermal root,
from the vibrissa of its muzzle,
wonder at asymmetric patterns
beneath the slide, how the hair
is surrounded by a vertical plexus
of nerve terminal, how it would look
duplicated in crimson
along the full circle of an A-line.

Nasturtium Seeds

You show me how the ripe seeds
from nasturtiums can be harvested,
pickled and eaten like capers.
I spy them through the windows
of a recycled jam jars, packed tight
in white wine vinegar, dense as pairs
of screw backed nineteen twenties earings.
Press your ear to the glass
and you will hear them slowly unscrewing,
hear fronds, tendrils scratching,
glorious and dammed,
those cute debutantes with stunner names,
Jet, Agate, Coral, Moonstone.

Toy Box Closed

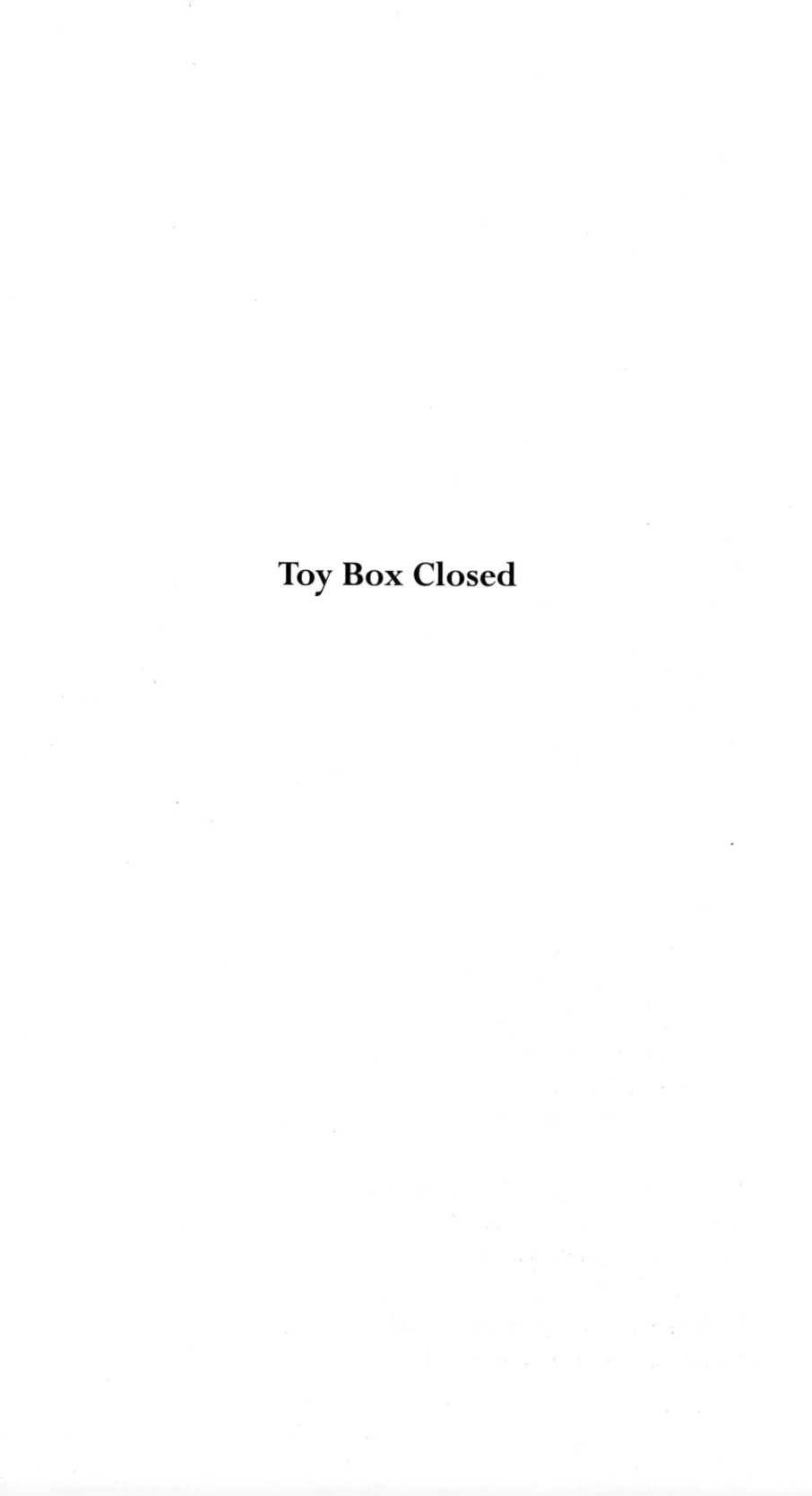

Hen

We had to teach you everything,
basic stuff, such as,
this is night, this is day,
this is a flower, a bush, a leaf.
Pointing with fingers
to a blot in the blue we told you,
this is the sun
and it hangs in what we just pointed to,
which sometimes we call blue,
which is the sky.
It's a bit like your old industrial light,
in the sense that it warms you.

Before we put you on the grass
we told you,
this is the grass,
and one of us held you,
while the other patted,
trawled the wild borders
for potential food to show to you,
as one of us ate,
first a spider then a fly.
Eventually we set you down,
though one of us kept an eye
on you through the window
as you sank, dragging your feet
underneath like a nit comb.

For a week you squatted, unsheathed,
flicking your beak like a blunt knife.
Then after a month, a tea cosy,
you warmed the earth.
We imagined you, as a ceramic pot,
lifting your top half-off like a lid,

a dozen sanitised eggs, barely touching.
Nowadays we see you,
as Elizabethan, scratching, grubbing,
ruffling your feathers,
taking out beetles and flies,
prone to hiding your eggs
as turtles do, afraid of the dawn,
the basket, drift of the early morning eye.

Magpie Husbandry

You say, 'as a country girl
I've seen magpies go back regularly
to a blackbirds.'
You see them watching,
day after day, week after week;
tending you might say,
in a hands-off sort of way,
till like a cash crop,
they're fat.

In Three Acts: Jane and Dorothy Fold Pieces of Pea Green Linen Printed With Cow Parsley

First step. There's the calculation,
soundness of good business sense.
In total six pieces to be sold,
six pieces of unequal length.
So six pieces priced accordingly,
two long enough for curtains
at a smallish window, four left
for accessories, room accoutrements.

Second step, Jane holds each piece
by finger and thumb, steps back
as they duplicate, Dorothy holds
each piece by finger and thumb,
steps back. Eye contact. Done.

Third step, involves obliteration
of a long crease that mars the middle.
Jane's led by the central crease,
as is Dorothy, so one yanks harder
than the other, till in the epicentre
they meet, trigger a series of quakes.
Although they're careful;
for a May wedding is coming,
not to completely overpower
or snag the corpulence of cow parsley.

A Turnip for Blue John

Outside Castleton,
inside the hillside near Mam Tor,
it's said that miners looking for lead
were first to strike fluorspar.
But Blue John myths die-hard;
such as the Romans
were the first to mine and export,
or the Iranians turned up the blue banded
as grave goods, or as was claimed,
two vases were excavated
from the ruins at Pompeii,
and the literary connection
tells us that Lawrence
once wrote in a letter to Ms Mansfield;
how in winter he traipsed
across the snowfields of Bonsal to Matlock
to buy her a piece,
wrapped it in his spotted handkerchief.
And this is all very well and good,
this history, but I've not got the money
to buy you a piece of antiquity,
so that's why land army-like
I'm pulling turnips from my plot,
tilting toward the earth I part the greens.
This white upper too has fourteen banding veins,
and I can count them ringed, purple,
wherever the precious moonlight falls.

Crich, With Sunbeams and Pewter Showers
for Pauline

As I climbed the steep hill to the tower,
I sensed you were behind,
chaffing at my heels in your black Mary Janes.
At the summit I told you how the dales
survived these past ten years or more,
and that place you spoke so often of,
ripening gold, is out there still
holding up against bleak winds,
pewter whipping showers, that you said
made women epic and men
grow very quick, very old in.

Tonight the universe sounds hollow,
though sequins of stars dare to tinkle
and carrion crewel around the ridge.
I say your name fast for fear it might frost,
but the wind, pitiful wind, cold as a spoon
shoves all sustenance back
and I fight it until I can no longer fight it,
for I am still in love with you, or the memory of you.

Margaret

Dorothy, don't mither so, I went willingly
and to a place of my own staking.
I settled up with the sexton
to be sunk beneath the yew,
denture of the dry stone wall.
Here no one worries about my moles,
sprouting hair, moult of my pubes,
or the white ring of cholesterol
that orbits the Blue John of my eyes.
I slumber at will, wake at will,
listen to the first crop of earlyies sprout,
sense the patter and pelt of rain,
white tension of the hare's winter coat.
Most, I want to enter my old cottage
with the cats only knowing,
gaily hear you say that once
you saw me on the open road.

The Door is Grey

They are painting the front door of the Estate cottage green, in keeping.
For two hours, scour of block on sandpaper, trireme of brush strokes,
clatter of letterbox, tap of signet ring on a galaxy of etched panels.
What with radio blasting, intermittent travel news, North West banter,
laugh of a man's man with his boy, more North West banter, above it all.
I remember one early summer morning, when the sky was cloudless,
                                                                                                    vulnerable.
I remember turning down the path and finding a peony bud felled by a slug.
I remember thinking, *Is it alive or dead? And if I'm quick,*
                                      water in a shallow dish should revive it.
What I'd give to see the bud raised crimson, see this cottage door stay grey,
on opening grey, walk straight in on plush crimson.
The day's work almost done, the creams and cutch of cow parsley trail,
beckon the nose of the dog, the man's man and his boy are happy with tea;
                                                                                                                               gesture so.
On the door, one patch of territory remains.
One patch of grey, swamped by the high drama of green.
Last night, flew out of the eaves handkerchiefs of bats to bid farewell.
For a year grey spelt out what might have been. Through the wooden gate
stone walls stood easy against grey, as did the stone plinth, window ledge,
as did purple plants, and purple did purple more and hollyhocks
swishing like sleigh bells, and sloe bushes turning wicked,
as did the winter jasmine, wild tobacco,
as did early evening, the marriage of honeysuckle with lilac,
of early evening black collapsed against the grey.
If one look alone could make it stay, the grey; the man's man and his boy
wouldn't go through with it if they knew.
One year it stood, grey as a helmet, mighty grey. In winter,
grey shouldered a holly wreath, summer a midsummer cushion.
This door is grey,
grey is this place's grain, grey coursing through wood,
this cottage's blood, and grey is how it must stay
as crimson pushes its way through peony bud,
though it be long gone.